A GUIDE DOG
PUPPY GROWS UP

A Guide Dog Puppy Grows Up

Written by Caroline Arnold

Photographs by Richard Hewett

HARCOURT BRACE JOVANOVICH, PUBLISHERS
SAN DIEGO NEW YORK LONDON

HBJ HG HP

Library of Congress Cataloging-in-Publication Data
Arnold, Caroline.
A guide dog puppy grows up/text by Caroline Arnold;
photographs by Richard Hewett. — 1st ed.
p.   cm.
Summary: Follows the career of a guide dog from
its raising as a puppy, through the training process,
to placement with a blind person.
ISBN 0-15-232657-X
1. Guide dogs — Training — Juvenile literature.
[1. Guide dogs — Training. 2. Dogs — Training.]
I. Hewett, Richard, ill.
II. Title.
HV1780.2.A76   1991
362.4'183 — dc20   90-5154

Designed by Richard Hewett and Katherine Tillotson

Printed in Singapore
First edition
A B C D E

ACKNOWLEDGMENTS

Guide Dogs for the Blind, Inc., is a nonprofit charitable organization dedicated to providing highly trained Guide Dogs to qualified men and women and training these men and women to work with the dogs. If you are interested in finding out more about this program, you can write to: Guide Dogs for the Blind, Inc., P.O. Box 151200, San Rafael, California 94915.

Guide Dogs for the Blind is one of several programs in the United States that train dogs to work with blind people. Other programs include The Seeing Eye dogs and International Guiding Eyes. In this book, the general term for such dogs is "dog guide"; dogs that are trained at Guide Dogs for the Blind are called "Guide Dogs."

We are grateful to everyone at Guide Dogs for the Blind for their enthusiastic cooperation on this project. In particular we thank Bruce Benzler, Chief Executive Officer, and Jennifer Conroy, Director of Development, for making this book possible. In addition we thank Joanne Ritter, Eric George, Terry Barrett, James Dugan, Craig Dietrich, DVM, Jeannette Davenport, Catherine Cadden, Cathleen Pitts, Brad Hibbard, Stacey O'Hara, Dana Cunningham, Pam Duryea, Jenny Brichta, Gina Johnson, and members of Class 485. We also thank puppy raisers Amy Duckert, Noelle and Brandon Nord, Virginia and Veronica Chitwood, and their families. Finally, we are especially thankful to Sister Anne Gelles and her dog, Honey. We could not have created this book without them.

HONEY COCKS HER EARS and peers through the fence. Footsteps are coming closer. Who can it be?

Perhaps a kennel worker is bringing more food. Perhaps someone is going to take her out for a walk. Or maybe it is a visitor wanting to learn more about Guide Dogs for the Blind.

Honey and the other puppies are part of a special program that teaches dogs how to help people who cannot see. During the next two years, the dogs will learn to lead blind people at home, at work, and wherever they want to go.

Honey and her kennel mates are purebred golden retrievers. In kennels nearby there are Labrador retriever puppies and German shepherd puppies. Although other kinds of dogs sometimes become guides, these are the only three breeds trained at Guide Dogs for the Blind. They make good guides because they are intelligent and seem to enjoy working with people.

More than three hundred dogs live at the Guide
Dogs for the Blind campus in San Rafael, California.
Sometimes Honey can see people working with older
dogs in the kennel corridor. Another section of the
kennel is for dogs waiting to begin their training.

In addition to the kennels, the campus includes a
dormitory, where the blind people live while learning
to work with their dogs, and an office building for the
Guide Dog staff.

Female dogs expecting puppies stay in a private area where they won't be disturbed by people or other dogs. Inside each of their kennels is a small television camera. Workers in the kennel kitchen can watch the mother dogs and their newborn puppies on television monitors. That way, they can keep track of the dogs without disturbing them. The puppies stay with their mothers for about six weeks. After that they are old enough to be on their own.

One day a volunteer worker comes to the kennel to get Honey. "What a lively puppy," she says. Between the ages of six and eleven weeks, Honey and the other puppies are tested once a week for alertness, general intelligence, and willingness to learn. Every dog has a different personality, and a puppy who is overly cautious or easily scared might not make a good guide.

In the puppy testing area, volunteers watch as Honey walks across a grating and looks at herself in a mirror. At first she thinks she is seeing another puppy, but when she tries to sniff it, all she meets is the cold mirror. Other tests include walking up stairs, hearing a loud noise, and playing with a new toy. Honey seems curious about everything, and the puppy testers agree that her responses are normal for a puppy of her age and experience.

A veterinarian and his staff look after all the dogs at Guide Dogs for the Blind. They check that the animals are healthy and that their bones are developing properly. Every puppy is routinely dewormed and vaccinated against dog diseases. Because the puppies will grow up to be working animals, it is important that physical or health problems will not prevent them from doing their jobs.

By the time Honey is twelve weeks old, she has successfully completed all of her puppy tests, and the veterinarian has declared her healthy. Now it is time for the second stage of preparing her to be a Guide Dog.

When a Guide Dog puppy is about three months old, it goes to live with a family. This family has volunteered to care for the puppy while it grows up.

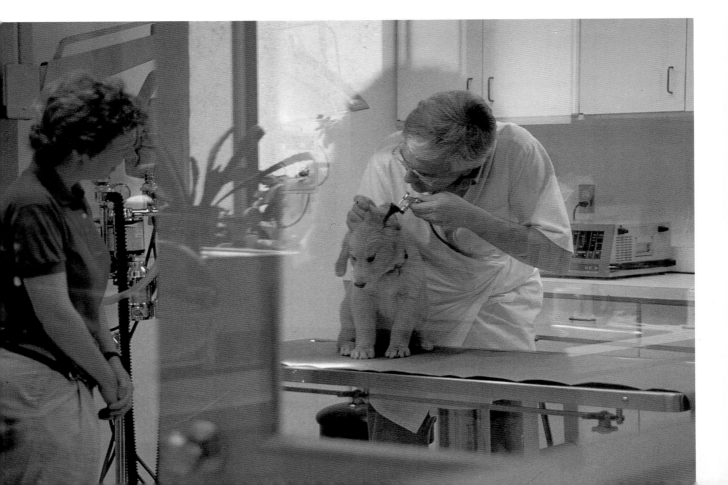

Honey's new home is with a nine-year-old girl named Amy and her family. Amy loves dogs and is eager to take care of one.

Like Amy, many puppy raisers are 4-H Club members. 4-H is a program that offers kids, usually in rural or suburban areas, the opportunity to do real-life projects in their homes, on farms, or in their communities. To become a puppy raiser, Amy filled out an application and had an interview with her 4-H project leader. The 4-H puppy placement department at Guide Dogs for the Blind gave Amy a pamphlet on puppy care and a chart to record Honey's growth and development. They also provided a dog collar showing the telephone number of Guide Dogs for the Blind and Honey's identification number in case she ever got lost.

Puppy raisers are responsible for the complete care of their dogs during the fifteen months or so they have them. They must housetrain and feed the puppies and keep them clean and healthy. The dog is treated as a family pet and learns to live with people. One of the things Honey enjoys most is playing with Amy and her friends.

During the time Amy has Honey, she keeps track of all their activities. Once a month they go to puppy-club meetings where they learn about puppy care and exchange news with other club members. Amy also teaches Honey simple commands so she will behave when they go out.

An important part of being a puppy raiser is getting the dog used to going out into the community, since this will be the dog's job when it is working with a blind person. So when Amy or her parents go to the super-market, bank, or even sometimes to work or school, they often take Honey with them. Ordinarily, animals cannot go into most places of business unless they are helping a handicapped person. Honey's green jacket tells people she is a Guide Dog puppy. When Honey wears the jacket, people often stop Amy to ask her about being a puppy raiser.

By the time Honey is a year and a half old, she has grown from a bouncy young puppy to a well-mannered adult dog. Her soft puppy coat has grown dark and silky, and her body has filled out to its grown-up shape.

In every way, Honey has become a real member of Amy's family, but soon the time comes for Honey to go back to the Guide Dog campus and begin her formal training. Amy knows she has played an important part in getting Honey ready to help a blind person, but she wishes Honey didn't have to go.

Amy's mother drives them to the Guide Dog campus. A staff member greets them at the car and explains the next stage of Honey's training. Before they leave, Amy gives Honey an extra hug. "I'll be back for your graduation," she says.

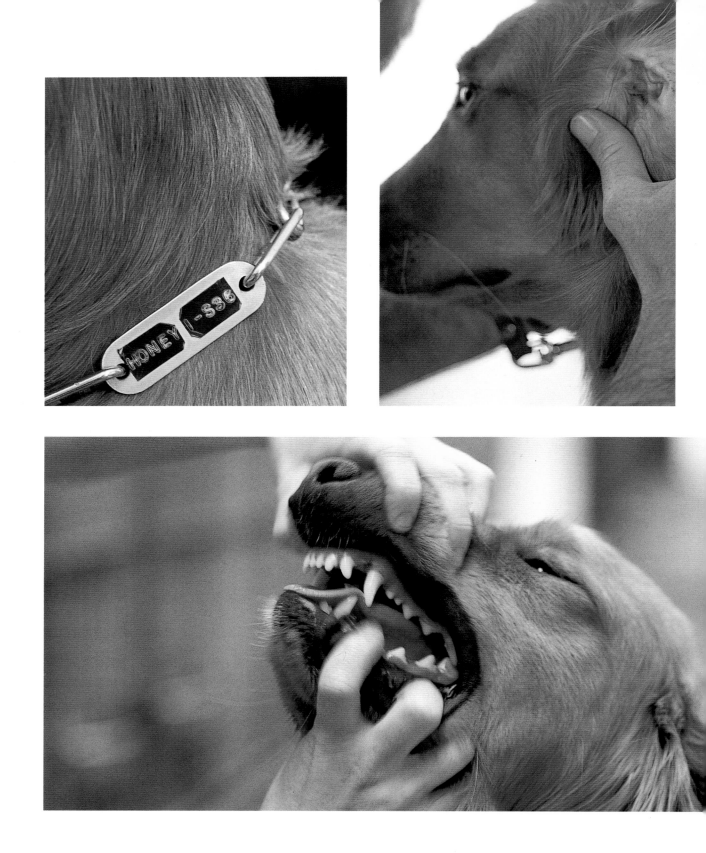

On her arrival at the Guide Dog campus, Honey is given a new collar and put into the receiving kennel. First an instructor checks her over and measures her height and weight. The veterinarian then gives Honey a thorough examination and X-rays her hips. He wants to make sure she will not develop any problems that could prevent her from walking properly.

If Honey did not measure up exactly to Guide Dog standards either physically or later in training, she would be made available for adoption. Amy would have the first chance to adopt her, but if for some reason Amy didn't want Honey, she would be offered to someone else. Even though a dog may not be quite right for working with a blind person, it can still make an excellent pet. Only about half of the dogs successfully complete every stage of the training and become Guide Dogs.

Both male and female dogs can become guides. A few of the dogs with especially good characteristics are used as breeders. These dogs live with families in the community except when it is time for breeding or when the females are due to give birth to puppies. The rest of the dogs are spayed or neutered because a dog guide cannot leave its blind partner to mate or have puppies.

After completing her checkup, Honey is moved into her new training kennel.

"Hello, Honey," says Terry, as he snaps a leash onto her collar. "Today you and I are going to start working together. If all goes well, you will be ready to be a guide in five or six months."

Terry is Honey's instructor, and every day he spends some time working with her. At first, Terry teaches Honey to sit and stay and to obey other basic commands. When Honey follows his instructions, he pats

her on the head and tells her she's a good dog. In all of her training, the only reward Honey needs is praise. Like most dogs, Honey is eager to please and learns quickly.

Each step of the training process helps Honey to learn skills she will need later when guiding a blind person. For instance, if a blind person drops something, the dog guide must know how to retrieve it. Early in her training, Honey learns to pick up an object and give it to Terry.

Each instructor is responsible for ten to fifteen dogs at a time. In the kennels next to hers, Honey can hear other dogs. She watches as instructors take these dogs out, one at a time, for their training sessions.

Three times a day, all the dogs in Honey's kennel are let out into a large fenced area where they can run freely and exercise. This is also a chance for the dogs to get to know each other. Dog guides must be comfortable around other animals so they do not become afraid or aggressive.

After several weeks of working Honey on a leash, Terry is ready to add harness training to her workout. Although Honey's 4-H jacket has helped her get used to wearing something on her back, it will take a while before she feels completely at ease in the new harness.

Until now, Honey has just walked beside Terry, but during the harness training sessions he has to teach Honey to pull him. Honey listens to Terry's commands to know whether she should pull him forward, turn left

or right, or stop. A dog guide is very intelligent, but it cannot know where a blind person wants to go without instructions. The dog and the person must work together to get safely to their destination.

Most of Honey's workouts are in downtown San Rafael. To get there, Terry takes her in a van along with several other dogs who are also being trained. When Honey's turn comes, she always jumps eagerly out of the van, ready to start working.

Six months go by quickly. In the final part of her training, Terry asks Honey to lead him on a walk as usual, but this time his eyes are covered by a blindfold. For safety, another trainer walks closely behind in case Honey makes a mistake. But the other trainer isn't needed this time because Honey guides Terry perfectly, just as she has been taught.

Honey has passed all her tests. Now she is ready to be placed with a blind person. Not all blind people want to have a dog guide. Some prefer to use a cane or to have other people guide them. Some do not like animals or don't want the responsibility of taking care of a dog. However, any legally blind person over the age of sixteen can apply to Guide Dogs for the Blind for a dog. After an extensive interview, those people ready for the responsibility of learning to live and work with a dog guide come to the Guide Dogs for the Blind campus.

Usually there are sixteen students in a class. During the four weeks of training they live in the dormitory together, two to a room. The students are of all ages and come from a variety of backgrounds. Some have been blind all their lives, and others have lost their sight more recently. While there are many different kinds and causes of blindness, all the students share the problem of how to get around without being able to see.

When Anne Gelles arrives on campus to begin her Guide Dog training, Terry greets her. He will be one of the instructors for her class. During the school year, Anne works as a teacher of blind children. Like many of them, she has been blind all her life. She wants a dog to help her get to and from her job. Like the other new students at Guide Dogs for the Blind, she is excited about getting a dog and at the same time a little worried about everything she will have to learn.

During their first few days on campus, the students learn their way around and get used to the daily routine. Even though they do not have dogs yet, they are learning how to give the correct commands. Terry pretends to be a dog named Juno as he teaches each student how to move and speak to a Guide Dog.

"I feel a little silly," says Anne, "because I know you aren't a real dog."

"I know," says Terry. "But I can tell you when you make a mistake, and a real dog can't."

Finally, on their fourth day on campus, the students are ready to meet their dogs for the first time.

That morning a kennel worker gives Honey a bath. "Today is an important day," she says, "and I want you to look your best."

When Honey is clean and dry, Terry comes to get her. Together they walk across the campus to meet Anne, who will be Honey's new partner.

Over the last six months, Terry and the other instructors have gotten to know all their dogs very well. Like people, each dog has its own personality. After meeting the new students and reviewing their needs and desires, Terry and other staff members carefully matched each person with one of the dogs.

"Hello, Anne," says Terry. "Here's Honey. She's a beautiful russet-colored golden retriever. I picked her especially for you because you both have lively personalities."

Anne laughs and reaches out to scratch Honey under the chin. Honey stretches her neck with pleasure.

"Hello, Honey," Anne says. "I can't wait to get to know you better. We're going to have fun together."

"Yes," says Terry. "It won't be easy at first. But, one month from now, you two are going to be a real team."

This is the first time any of the students in Anne's training group have worked with a dog. The students must learn not only how to work with their dogs but also how to take care of them.

Anne finds out how much and how often to feed Honey and when to take her out to relieve herself. She also learns how to keep Honey clean and when to take her to the vet for checkups. By taking care of her physical needs, Anne shows Honey that she cares about her.

For the remaining three and a half weeks of training, Honey will live in Anne's room along with Anne's roommate and her dog.

Classes begin every morning after breakfast. Sometimes the students listen to lectures or have discussions with staff members, but more often they board buses and go into town. The group usually gathers in the lounge of the Guide Dog building near the San Rafael business district. From there the student-and-dog teams go out to practice their skills. An instructor supervises each trip. Getting everything right the first time is not easy, and as the students wait their turns they share their problems with each other.

At first the students memorize and follow a short route around the block. Each day their walks grow longer and more complicated as they become familiar with the area. Gradually they learn how to go around barriers, into elevators, and up and down stairs. They enter offices, grocery stores, and banks. The instructors help the students learn the kinds of skills they will need when they go home with their dogs.

People in San Rafael are used to seeing Guide Dogs almost every day. A dog guide can be recognized by its special harness. Even though the animal may look friendly, it is not a good idea to pet it without first asking permission from its blind partner. A dog in harness is at work, and petting might distract it.

One of the most important skills for a blind person to learn is how to cross a street safely. Whenever Anne and Honey come to a corner, Anne has to decide whether they will go right, left, or straight ahead. Whenever they have to cross a street, Honey leads Anne to the curb and stops until Anne has found the edge with her foot. Then Honey waits while Anne listens to the traffic noise. When Anne can hear that the cars have stopped and she decides it is safe to cross, she signals Honey to lead her across the street.

Dogs cannot tell the difference between red and green lights, so Honey does not watch traffic signals when she guides Anne. Honey does watch traffic, however, and she will refuse to take Anne across a street if she sees a car coming. This is called "intelligent disobedience," and it is one way Honey makes sure she and Anne are safe.

Finally, after four weeks of hard work, the students and their dog partners finish their training. Graduation ceremonies are held every fourth Saturday and are attended by family, friends, and interested people in the community.

On the morning of graduation day, Anne and Honey wake up early. Excitement is in the air as the students talk about their future plans. After lunch, Anne puts on her favorite dress and packs her last few belongings. Then she sits down to wait for one of the staff to tell her Honey's puppy raiser has arrived. Soon she hears a knock on the door.

"They're here," says Terry. "Let me bring you to meet them."

Anne, Honey, and Terry walk down the corridor toward Amy and her mother. As soon as Amy sees them, she runs forward and throws her arms around Honey's neck.

"I'm so glad to see you again!" she cries.

Terry introduces Amy and her mother to Anne. Amy is eager to hear about Anne's job and how Honey will go with her to school. Anne enjoys learning from Amy what Honey was like as a puppy.

Soon it is time for all the students to take their seats on the stage. Amy and Honey wait with the other puppy raisers and their dogs in the lounge. When Anne's turn comes to graduate, one of the staff members helps her step forward. Amy then leads Honey out the door and across the stage to the microphone. She hands Honey's leash to Anne, saying, "To Anne Gelles, I now present Honey. I know she will be one of the best Guide Dogs ever."

"Thank you," says Anne. "I'm proud to have her."

When the ceremony is finished, Anne will leave the Guide Dogs for the Blind campus and take Honey home. Although Anne is looking forward to her new life with Honey, she is sad to be leaving her new friends. She also wants to say goodbye to Amy.

"I'm so glad we could meet," Anne says to Amy. "You did a great job of helping Honey to grow up."

"I miss her," Amy says. "But I'm glad you have her. I know she'll be happy."

After graduation, Anne and the other students go back to their homes. Some return to their old jobs; others begin new careers. Guide Dog graduates work at many different kinds of jobs. They are lawyers, social workers, newspaper reporters, piano tuners, or almost anything else.

Like other blind people and their dog guide partners, Anne and Honey will enjoy the special kind of love and companionship that comes from living and working together. Most dog guides can work until they are about ten years old. When a Guide Dog retires, its blind partner may keep it as a pet, or the dog may be adopted by its puppy raiser or someone else.

Anne feels very lucky to have Honey. She knows the hard work of many people contributed to their success as a team. The four weeks of training were not easy, but Anne feels confident that they are off to a good start. As each day goes by, Anne and Honey will continue to learn from each other, and they can look forward to many happy years together.